Cut Both Ways

Peaks & Valleys
of a Passionate Relationship
Expressed Through
Poetry

By P.S. Rowland

© 2015 P.S. Rowland

This book is copyright under the Berne Convention
No reproduction without permission
All rights reserved.

ISBN: 978-1-910115-36-7

Prepared for publication by LionheART Publishing House
www.lionheartgalleries.co.uk
Cover design by Shaina Longstreet
www.yourampersandstudio.com
Cover photo by Alexandre Vanier

The right of P.S. Rowland to be identified as the author of this work has been asserted by her in accordance with sections 77 and 78 of the Copyright, Designs and Patents Act 1988.

Dedicated to the one who has opened my heart to emotions I never knew existed.

"I don't want good, and I don't want good enough, I want can't sleep, can't breathe without your love."

Hunter Hayes

Contents

Foreword i
Introduction iii
Cut Both Ways 1
Merry-Go-Round 2
Trust 3
Convergence 4
Heart to Heart 5
The Thread That Binds 6
Armor 7
Symbolic of Infinity 8
Moments 9
Gridlocked 10
Collision 11
Revolution 12
Renew by Death 13
Misguided 14
Pressure 15
The Mask 16
Forks 18
I Dream a Dream 19
Heat 20
The Puzzle 20
The Beginning of the End 21
Ecstasy 22
Self-Destruction 22
Woven Together 23
Thump − Senryu 24
Superlative Desire 24
Destined 25
Judgment − Haiku 25

Long Suffering	26
Beating	27
Senses	28
Intoxication – Senryu	28
Math of Love	29
Silent – Senryu	29
Broken – Senryu	30
Selfless	30
Aggregator	31
Awaken – Senryu	31
Never Part With the Ace of Hearts	32
Love Is	33
Miss Me	34
US – 10W	34
Power of Love	35
Treason	36
Despair – 10W	37
Two = One	37
Love/Hate	38
Senses of Passion	39
Clarity – 10W	39
Chances – Senryu	40
Lessons	40
Kindred Spirits	41
Self-Doubt	42
Executed	43
Strategic	44
Self-Loathing – Senryu	45
Severed – Senryu	45
Loop – Haiku	45
Dive – Senryu	46
Craving – Senryu	46
Abstruse	46
My Everything	47
Veni Vidi Vici	48

Realism 49
Memories 50
Damaged 51
Undeniable Love 52
Conviction – 10W 53
Maze 53
Absolute – 10W 54
Suffocation – Senryu 54
Dazed 55
Obsessed – Senryu 56
She / He 56
Disturbance 57
Crucible 58
Turmoil 59
Balm 59
Vow 60
Him – 10W 60
Lambent 61
Hunger – Senryu 61
Sinking 62
Assassin - Senryu 62
Duel 63
Molten Love – Senryu 63
Bite – Senryu 64
Gravity – 10W 64
Beautiful Confusion 65
Grounded – 10W 66
Soul Deep – 10W 66
Shield – Senryu 66
My Protector 67
Focus 68
Ponder 69
Heaven 69
Fractions 70
Yo-Yo – 10W 70

Lukewarm – Senryu 71
Osmosis – 10W 71
Soulmuch 71
Double Nickels 72
Reverse Black Widow – Senryu 72
Grasshopper – 10W 73
Cleansing – Triolet 73
Voltaic – Triolet 74
Limitless – Senryu 74
Tutu – Triolet 75
Vision – 10W 75
Leather & Lace 76
Blind Touch – 10W 77
Serenity – Senryu 77
Rapture – Triolet 78
Kinesics – 10W 78
Complete – Triolet 79
Hearken – Senryu 79
Hopelessly Devoted – Triolet 80
Frost Bite – Senryu 80
Calculating 81
Heart Throb – Senryu 81
Renewal 82
Comfort – Triolet 82
Scorch – Senryu 83
Enliven 83
Rhythmic Love – Triolet 84
Butterfly Kisses – Senryu 84
The One 85
Falling Into Place – Triolet 86
Soothing – 10W 86
Fragility 87
Sated 87
Perfect Storm 88
Revive 88

"When" – Senryu	89
A New Song – Triolet	89
Shilly-Shally	90
In Pieces – Triolet	91
Spirits – Triolet	91
Wanderlust	92
Transform – Senryu	92
Insanity – Triolet	93
Exposed – Triolet	93
Babydoll – Triolet	94
United – Triolet	94
Theater Of War	95
Divided – Senryu	95
Cutting – Senryu	96
Exhaustion – Triolet	96
Good Morning My Love	97
Other Books by P.S. Rowland	99
Acknowledgements	100

Foreword

Cut Both Ways will carry you along a beautiful path of love, grief, elation, inspiration, and passion. A journey not many experience in their lifetime; delving deep within the emotions of two creative, romantic, intense, and passionate soulmates. The author demonstrates great skill, allowing the reader to feel the ecstasy, excitement, and disturbance portrayed in each poem. Stirring the desires of the heart and soul, which come into play when two beautiful souls are more than just in love, more than in a relationship, where two become one. The dynamics and intensity of these poems will transport you into a world so precious, it will take your breath away.

P.S. Rowland

Introduction

In a relationship more often than not, both parties are not passionate people. Passionate, not necessarily in a romantic sense, but about life in general; feeling strongly about goals, interests, ideas and yes, dreams and love.

Usually one is a taker, one a giver. The old adage "opposites attract", or do they? This collection of works will delve into the life of a relationship where both individuals are extremely artistic, intense, passionate about life, and fierce about love.

P.S. Rowland

Cut Both Ways

P.S. Rowland

Cut Both Ways

Double-edged love is the thrill he instills in my soul.
Double-edged love is the stab in my chest when I've disappointed him.
Double-edged love is the yearning I feel in my gut when he looks at me.
Double-edged love is the hurt in my bones when he misunderstands my words.
Double-edged love is the warmth of his body against mine making us one.
Double-edged love is the sadness I have in my heart because I am confused.
Double-edged love is the smile he gives me that shines through my eyes.
Double-edged love is the hate I feel for myself when I betray him.
Double-edged love is the passion ripping through my body as I inhale his scent.
Double-edged love is the realization that he is mine, and yet he is not.
Double-edged love is the flutter inside my being when I feel his proximity.
Double-edged love is the emptiness when he leaves.
Double-edged love is the realization that ours is the love of a lifetime.
Double-edged love is our near death, because of our love.

Merry-Go-Round

Searing upwards
at lightning speed,
plummeting downward,
dashing my needs.
Mind is a blender,
heart is in turmoil
clarity is needed,
before the spoil.
Love is complex,
not black and white.
Choices are made,
not always right.

Trust

Tender is the heart.
Breakable is the soul.
I give to you my trust,
and you break it like a bowl.

Picking up the pieces.
Wishing I would mend.
You try to say the words,
but I fear I see a trend.

My spirit is downcast,
as low as it can go.
I cannot stay the course,
if my lover is the foe.

How to trust again,
remove pictures from my mind.
I long for what once was,
when my eye to pain was blind.

Convergence

I give you my soul,
as you breathe life
into my existence.
The gentle caress
of your eyes
releases tension,
building since our last encounter.
You fill, and replenish
all that is lacking
in my world without you.
Two shooting stars
colliding in utter bliss.

Heart to Heart

Beautiful each moment,
precious in my heart.
Now that it's all over,
I want a fresh new start.

Please come back and hold me.
Look into my eyes.
My world is not complete,
without you by my side.

The air I breathe is you.
You keep my soul alive.
Your love is what sustains me,
without it I would die.

Until your next touch,
I hold you close in mind.
Our love we share together,
will stand the test of time.

The Thread That Binds

You're the center of my world.
My every breath,
my every thought.
The pain I caused you
has destroyed my viscera,
along with my heart.
What you feel, I feel.
The ache that binds us together
will make us stronger.
Never have two lost souls,
been destined to search out,
find, and connect, as ours.
I will not let go.
I cannot let go.
you have wedged yourself
into my heart, and have
sewn it shut, to be there for an eternity.

Armor

Many hearts have broken,
some may never heal.
I wish I had protected mine,
so this burn I did not feel.

To guard against this pain,
is impossible it seems.
It feels so good at first,
like a fairytale of dreams.

Each encounter is more thrilling.
I crave more with every touch.
Soon my heart is impaired,
depending on you as my crutch.

Fragmented I am without you.
You are the strength within my soul.
If you walked away tomorrow,
I would never again be whole.

Symbolic of Infinity

Words burst forth
from my heart,
as I think of you.
Emotions new to me,
a seasoned woman,
whose soul has been awakened.
The nature of your tenderness,
understanding and zest,
have aroused my passion for life.
Missed opportunities
of happiness
have slipped by me.
Going through the motions
for years on end,
not realizing what was lacking.
You've infused my essence
with liveliness,
bubbles and rainbows.
You fill my lungs with air,
breathe in, breathe out.
My very existence
resides within
your eyes and heart.
You transfuse and drench
my vital force,
as you saturate me with your love.
The intensity of our devotion,
is reinforced,
each time I peer into your eyes.
From here to infinity
dust to dust,
we ride side by side.

Moments

The morning chill
feels as desolate
as my heart.
Loneliness has struck,
like the sound of silence.
Five days' time has passed
since I've held your eyes,
and you've kissed my lips.
I shall wander
through the day,
with you dripping
from my heart and mind.
I lie in waiting
counting my breaths
till the next moment
we will claim.

Gridlocked

The ache of one's heart
reaches to the pit of the stomach.
Uneasiness clouds the mind.
Floating between two worlds.
Unsure how to navigate
to the one you desire.
How can there be
so much pain,
amongst immense love and passion.
Choose one, making happy,
hurting the one left behind.
Releasing one life,
building anew, alone,
aside from each other.
When does one stay true
to thyself?
Gridlocked between two worlds,
rendering each of them incomplete.

Collision

Waiting for the shadows
to clear within my mind.
To have a day about me,
and do not feel I'm blind.

The complexities of life,
are jumbled in a pile.
Sifting through the refuse,
to navigate an aisle.

The heart and mind at war,
the scrimmage to the end.
One will win the battle,
the other will need to mend.

Right and wrong are present.
The answer I should know.
The first will breed resentment,
the second an inner glow.

Others do pass judgment,
as I ignore their admonition.
In matters of the heart,
do we know the disposition?

Working out our own path,
each must do alone.
Giving careful thought
to the ones you have at home.

Revolution

The pain and the struggle,
the battle between light and dark,
past and future,
robs you from enjoying the present.
Reflecting on what was,
dreaming about what could be,
leaves nothing for today, but tears.
In want of what is not yours,
shaking the foundation of what is.
Grasping at imagery
you've exaggerated in your mind.
A merry-go-round of emotions,
too difficult to pass through.
Numbness and anxiety
control your body and soul simultaneously.
A vicious cycle,
you're unable to fracture.
The mind is strong,
the heart is weak,
and yet it continues to prevail,
no matter the consequence.

Renew by Death

Loving what once was
rekindle that within.
Where to start is the question,
oh where do I begin?

The need to start out slow,
putting forth a struggle.
Close my eyes and remember
how my emotions I do juggle.

At first it will be awkward,
to force what isn't there.
I'll try to persevere,
and give it up to prayer.

In time my heart will mend,
at least that's what I'm told.
The memory will linger,
until the day I'm cold.

How do I go back,
to a love that once was there,
and forget about the one in my heart,
without causing such despair?

One day at a time they say.
Get up, get dressed, and breathe.
Mind over emotions and thought,
my broken heart it will sheathe.

Misguided

Tension of the heart,
pulling oh so taut.
Emotions running high,
with the troubles that you brought.

Heaviness sets in,
pushing out the good.
Sorrow strikes you down,
as others said it would.

Deception breeds disaster,
don't fool yourself on this.
You'll lose what you were after,
not gain the wedded bliss.

Let go of what is wrong,
remember what you have.
Give into what is right,
let it heal like a soothing salve.

Pressure

Silence is the sound around me.
Lonely in my thoughts I do perish.
Working through the wonders of my life.
The good, the bad, and the indecision.
Age and maturity have not necessarily progressed
in the right direction.
Complications have crept in,
and have rendered me confused.
My thoughts involve many around me.
Touching them in a variety of ways.
So much lies on my shoulders.
The future of others' happiness,
is at my mind's fingertips.
Seeking guidance in all I do,
and yet resisting the answers.
So much of today lost in yesterday,
and tomorrow, entangled with emotions.
Resolutions may never come by choice,
but by force.

The Mask

We live, we love, we die
We breathe in goodness
Exhale badness
We fool ourselves with
What life is
We do bad, but see good
We do good, but see bad
Trial and error
Pain and sorrow
Spattered with moments of joy
We live in yesterday, and tomorrow
But rarely in today
Wishing all along we knew
The right path
Lessons given, and yet not learned
Repeated processes
Throughout life
Where we still fail
Time and time again
Attempts to glimpse at the person
You are within
All the while you live as the person
Others see you as
Darkness settles into the
Deepest places and
Refuses to leave
Light bounces off and
Barely touches the soul

Cut Both Ways

Passion inside longing
To burst forth, and yet
There is no safe place to do so
Trapped within ourselves
By the expectations of others
We live, we love, we die

Forks

Wandering life's path,
windy as it is.
Twirling through the journey before us,
in hopes of passing the quiz.

Hearts and minds split,
speaking foreign talk.
They rarely understand each other
the words don't match the walk.

Decisions become harder,
than what to wear to school.
Many of our choices,
leave us looking like a fool.

On this road of life,
a fork is now in front.
Where to go from here,
is the answer you must hunt.

I Dream a Dream

I sit and dream a dream
one so perfect, and only for me.
With sun on my face,
grass between my toes,
my hand in yours,
forever more.

No pressures, no worries,
just happiness and love.
Together we are,
like a well-fitted glove.

Lavishing good
on all those around,
Negativity is impossible
if ever to be found.

This is the way of life
I dream in my heart.
Creating the perfect plan,
waiting till it starts.

Cold left behind,
shed sweater and shoes.
I feel you beside me,
all I need is you.

Heat

The caress of your words against my skin.
The feel of your love as it deepens within.

The passion in your eyes as they bore through my soul.
Our inner connection is what makes me feel whole.

Your wanton desire laid bare before me.
My moans in your ear are my heartfelt plea.

The need for more as our bodies entwine.
Blending into one, I'm yours and you're mine.

The Puzzle

To know him is to love him.
To love him is to feel him.
To feel him is to hear him.
To hear him is to touch him.
To touch him is pure heaven.

The Beginning of the End

The beginning of the end,
settles deep within her heart.
The love she felt back then,
turned to jealousy that smarts.

A beautiful journey it was,
full of passion, love and desire.
Yet soon his love was controlling,
and he viewed her as a liar.

She tried to show her love,
prove he was her whole star.
It appeased him for a moment,
yet left her with a scar.

Markings on her heart,
grew deeper over time.
Each beating left her fragile,
with a higher rock to climb.

Piece by piece he chiseled,
chipping away at her soul.
Soon he had what he wanted:
a cracked and empty bowl.

Ecstasy

His presence is her air,
as he gently strokes her hair.
Tucked within his arms,
She knows she's safe from harm.
The passion created from him,
burrows deep within her skin.
The intensity of their love,
is what others wish and dream of.
How rare this union is,
as she thanks the gods she's his.

Self-Destruction

Deceit burrows holes within your soul,
creating cavities you will never begin to fill.
Chipping away at your self-worth.
Self-destruction is near at hand,
compliments of yourself.

Woven Together

The journey's been a dream,
a perfect fairytale.
One of gentle caresses,
a love that will not fail.

Where minds and souls connect,
without any effort at all.
Emotions of the heart,
causing us to be enthralled.

The story's quite unique.
It's different than the others.
Worlds will have to crash,
in order to be together.

The link that intertwines us,
is impossible to sever.
The thread that binds our hearts,
is here to stay forever.

Thump – Senryu

Beating in my soul
One music note at a time
Is your heart in mine?

Superlative Desire

The longing, and the ache.
The beating of my heartbreak.
The love in your eyes.
As blue as the skies.
The tenderness in your touch.
That means oh so much.
The commitment in your heart,
That's been there from the start.
Just a few of the things,
to my heart you do bring.
Just a few of the pieces,
Which never do cease.
Increasing my love for you,
that is deep, honest and true.

Destined

With the touch of his lips he writes her future on his heart.
An end that was destined right from the start.
External love all wrapped up together.
All tangled up in a beautiful forever.

Judgment – Haiku

Eyes peering through fog
Damp within my aching heart
Do I live or die?

Long Suffering

Change of seasons in the heart.
So polar opposite from the start.
Absence they say makes the heart grow fonder.
Experience shows, it drifts over yonder.
With space to reflect
on where you should be.
The answer is clear,
it's you, and it's me.
The calmness you've had
has lifted a load.
As it turns out,
you chose the right road.
Excitement you'll miss,
sad days will come.
So focus on the positive,
and happy will be some.

Beating

To care for another's heart,
is a weighty responsibility.
Delicate, and oh so fragile,
in your hands is where I long to be.
The desperation in your eyes,
the wanton looks, pleas and cries.
I fear the pain I will cause you,
Is what I'll need to start anew.
You've fallen hard for me I know.
And die you will if I should go.
Another loves me as you do.
One will win, and one will lose.
For me the pain is there for both.
But one was first to hear my oath.
To care for another's heart
Is a weighty responsibility.
Delicate and oh so fragile,
and has fallen right on me.

Senses

I hear his every thought.
I see deep within his soul.
I taste the love he gives,
upon me, he does bestow.
I touch his hardened body,
and quivers run their course.
The power wrapped around me,
is a hot and sensual force.

Intoxication — Senryu

Heat upon my lips
Hot breath across my body
Ecstasy complete

Math of Love

Standing four
Divided by two
If two were gone
It's me and you

Silent – Senryu

Heavy is my heart
The sound within is silent
I could write all day

Broken – Senryu

Dripping with sorrow
My core is bleeding within
Patch me with your love

Selfless

Live out of yourself
for those you love.
Live in their hearts,
to show what you're made of.
Love not in vain.
Love not for your own gain.
You gave your heart away,
work it gently,
so it doesn't break away.

Aggregator

His presence is all I need.
His words are on what I feed.
His touch is what uplifts me.
In his eyes it's the love I see.
His scent is the air I respire.
The elixir which brings on desire.
He's the total sum of life for me.
It is he, I, and we.

Awaken – Senryu

Touch my soul with love
With your lips resurrect me
Hearts throbbing as one

Never Part With the Ace of Hearts

The risk to love,
is a painful gamble.
Opening one's heart,
to be nurtured or scrambled.
A purposeful decision,
some do seek.
Glancing through the crowd,
for a hopeful peek.
Yet others dance through life,
busy and distracted.
Choosing one at random
by reason of attraction.
Soon to find loneliness,
sadness, and regret.
Empty souls, dreaded nights,
is what they soon beget.
The key to love,
is not to look.
Or dream and fantasize,
of lovers in a book.
When your heart is ready,
your soulmate will arrive.
Beautiful and tender,
and bring your soul alive.
Don't settle or be rushed,
listen to your heart.
You'll recognize your soulmate,
and never have to part.

Love Is

Love is ~ His scent when he walks through the door.
Love is ~ The sexy crooked smile he sends my way the moment he catches sight of me.
Love is ~ The warmth and depth of passion in his eyes as he bores through my soul.
Love is ~ The sound of his voice when he whispers, "God I love you."
Love is ~ The shivers that rush through my body at the mere brush of his hand against mine.
Love is ~ The pure intensity when he hugs me so long and hard that my breath comes from his lungs.
Love is ~ The fever that breaks out the moment his lips touch mine, a sickness I never want cured.
Love is ~ The time he spends singing lyrics to me from love songs because they are "us".
Love is ~ The silent moments that pass as we trace each line on each other's faces, lost in the passion of what we see.
Love is ~ Hours of talking and laughing over nothing, everything, and anything in between.
Love is ~ The secrets and intimate moments behind closed doors.
Love is ~ A once in a lifetime love affair with your soulmate
Love is ~ US

Miss Me

Heavy in my heart,
my feelings seem to be.
Press me to your chest,
and make sweet love to me.
You are in my soul,
your heartbeat is in me.
Look me in the eye,
and set my body free.

US – 10W

His passion
pushed forth
into her soul
for an eternity

Power of Love

I glance into your eyes,
they catch and reel me in.
My heart leaps into yours,
how can this be a sin?

Your soul is mine in kind,
my words are yours that speak.
Our love is intertwined,
my heart is yours to keep.

I pray that I be heard,
that love will find a way,
to make this union work,
for here I want to stay.

Please bend upon your knees.
Let's close our eyes together.
A love as perfect as this,
is surely meant forever.

P.S. Rowland

Treason

Uneasiness devours me.
Unsettling thoughts drown me.
Nervousness becomes me.
Losing myself one emotion at a time.
Confusion has taken control of me.
I fight to understand.
I hate the person I've become,
and yet cherish the life you created within me.
Double-edged sword,
sharper than I ever imagined.
I don't recognize who I am anymore.
And yet you've taught me more,
about myself than I ever thought possible.
I live and breathe for you.
Yet I am killing you.
We suffer at each other's hands.
I long to hold you and tell you,
everything will be OK.
But we both know that is just another,
one of our many lies.
The one truth,
I love like I've never loved before.
Because of your magic touch,
to my heart and soul.
Your heart and soul will forever be,
inside mine.

Despair – 10W

My heart
is full,
and yet,
it's empty
in vain

Two = One

He cares for her,
with protective armor.
She senses he
would let no one harm her.
He carries her heart,
close to his own.
She's flesh of his flesh,
and bone of his bones.
Together they ride,
on the wings of life.
He's bound and determined,
to make her his wife.

Love/Hate

He breeds in her love.
Yet insecurity,
pushing the boundaries
of affection versus pity.
His love can lift her,
toward the sky.
Then, dash her to pieces,
crushed, left to die.
Uncertainty flows
throughout her core.
She never knows,
if he'll purr or roar.
The slow decay
of her self-worth.
His manipulation
of her rebirth.
She now is new,
just how he likes.
But gone she is
from her own life.

Senses of Passion

Do you, or don't you have passion?
Do you love it, or hate it?
Take it, or leave it?
Feel it, or fake it?
Earn it, or steal it?
See it, or shun it?
Smell it, or exhale it?
Hear it, or ignore it?
Taste it, or spew it?
Hold it, or throw it?
Do you or don't you have passion
for life?
Middle ground is murky.

Clarity – 10W

The mind's eye
opened
and finally
touched the
heart's vision.

Chances – Senryu

Bore my soul to you
Shaky, fragile, broke in two
Only for rebuff

Lessons

In her heart she feels,
lonely, lost, and torn.
She tries to share her pain,
yet sorrow and fear were born.
Her plight is her own doing,
she chose this path to walk.
Her lover has betrayed her,
in deeds and idle talk.
A lesson there is to learn,
somewhere in all this pain.
Muddling through the emotions,
she hopes herself to gain.

Kindred Spirits

Mending of the hearts,
blending of the minds.
Your words caress my soul,
and to me they do bind.

When doubt creeps into darkness,
blinding out the light.
You cover me with kisses,
and make all matters right.

You read each silent word,
written upon my heart.
You know me inside out,
you have right from the start.

You handle me with care,
like a fragile crystal vase.
You stroke me with your eyes,
as I feel it on my face.

Never has there been,
a fusion such as ours.
Not in heaven, or on earth,
we are higher than the stars.

Self-Doubt

Tonight I rock myself to sleep.
The pain I feel I will not keep.
My heart will close so it won't break.
My tears will flow for my own sake.
The strong are weak,
and the weak are strong.
For this I've known, all along.
Which one I am I do not know,
for one will stay, and one will go.
In search of peace, and
calmness of mind,
I peer inside for the answer to find.
In search for what the truth shall be,
for you are you, and I am me.

Executed

The pain is crippling within.
Lord help me, and save me again.
I'm shattered and lost in my soul.
For only one can make me whole.
He's now gone away from my world.
I lay here in ache, sobbing and curled.
The life within me was you.
Only "US" of our tenderness knew.
Together we stood strong in love.
Together like two turtle doves.
Now broken and falling apart.
No longer one, but two broken hearts.

Strategic

Absorbed into my core he is,
weaving my thoughts and feelings.
I attempt to float away,
yet he's master over my dealings.
My mind declares, "Break free."
I'm prisoner in my own soul.
Masterfully he turns the key,
and molds me like a potter's bowl.
The battle within myself,
is at best a worn-out record.
Playing over and over again,
leaving everything black and white checkered.
He directs me like a pawn.
He's stronger than I am.
In matters of the heart,
I do know he's my man.

Self-Loathing – Senryu

Hate within yourself
For all your ugly movements
Stop being selfish

Severed – Senryu

Hit within the heart
Bleeding through the cracks you cut
Healing on my own

Loop – Haiku

Shadows cast aside
Cotton showering to earth
Sun extracts the dank

Dive – Senryu

My zest is lacking
Your virtue lifts me higher
Don't let me plummet

Craving – Senryu

Quench my desires
Caress the innermost me
Paint inside the vault

Abstruse

Green vapors float to the platform,
across the abyss of happiness.
Heat strokes the air levitating
above darkness.
Dampness greets skin, smoothly,
filtering glimpses of satin across glass.
The movement shuddering, gyrating,
black against black, resulting
in a kaleidoscope of finito.

My Everything

He is: The beat within my heart.
He is: The reason my day starts.
He is: The flow within my veins.
He is: The balm that heals my pain.
He is: The strength within my reason.
He is: My spring, summer, my season.
He is: The flame within my eye.
He is: The reason that I try.
He is: The vigor that pulls me through.
He is: The one that makes me new.
He is: The spirit within my form.
He is: The heat that keeps me warm.
He is: Everything that is me.
He is: The one who holds my key.

Veni Vidi Vici

You're the man who sends ripples of desire
through my body with just a thought.

You're the man who looks at me,
so deeply, and with so much passion,
that I melt into your arms.

You're the man who listens to me,
and talks to me for hours on end,
and yet we never run out of anything
to say.

You're the man who tenderly touches my heart,
soul, and body at just the right moments.

You're the man who can change all that in a nanosecond
to deep, intense passion, because you know that's what I need.

You're the man who is in my soul.
You are my soulmate.

Realism

Years have slipped on by.
There are wrinkles by my eyes.
Time is not my friend,
more years it will not lend.
I'm finally living life,
although it comes with strife.
The dreams that I have had,
and wanted oh so bad,
have finally come to be,
and set my soul afree.
Yet months and years
are few now.
Energy has waned.
I've wasted so much time,
and now it's all in vain.

Memories

Excitement and thrills,
of what's to come.
Three days so free,
to spiral undone.
Sun and blue skies,
caressing our skin,
with knees in the breeze,
we don't care where
we've been.
Smiles and laughter,
and fancy party drinks.
A relaxing time,
where nobody thinks.

Damaged

Assaulted and twisted,
snapped in two.
Bloated and tender,
now black and blue.
Weakened and useless
for a time it will be.
Weeks on end,
before I can flee.
Trapped, lying low,
trying to mend.
Time dragging on,
I need my best friend.
He cares for my soul,
my heart he does cherish.
My body he caresses,
so it will not perish.

Undeniable Love

His love has come my way.
In my heart, he is here to stay.
Every moment I have with him,
fills my heart, right to the brim.
His gentleness with me,
is like waves upon the sea.
My moments in his arms,
is my time away from harm.
He breathes life into me,
setting my mind so free.
The visions in my head,
which do begin to spread.
He's precious to my life,
as he makes it oh so bright.
Without him I'd be hollow,
a slow death soon to follow.

Conviction – 10W

Trust in my heart
and ecstasy will
be yours forever

Maze

Love within my heart
anxiety in my interior.
I ponder every day,
what could be your ulterior?
I long to settle and trust.
To be certain of my decision.
I fear the path I take,
is heading toward collision.
My life is in your hands.
I'm putty against your soul.
I trust you'll do what's right,
to make our future whole.

P.S. Rowland

Absolute – 10W

Cherish my every breath
until your heart
has consumed me.

Suffocation – Senryu

Trapped inside your needs
Drowning in my shallow lungs
Get off my chest please

Ideations wax and wane
within my brain.

Certainty is mine until
it is not.

Clouds floating behind my eyes
block my view.

Attempting to blink them away
is futile.

Swallowing back the answers
to the questions.

Questions which have no answers
I choke on.

Tomorrow brings a new day
of confusion.

Ideations which wax and wane
within my brain.

Obsessed – Senryu

Passion seeps inside
Surging through my veins for you
Fill me with your soul

She / He

Lost within herself,
he finds her in his heart.
She struggles to get out,
he's loved her from the start.
She's shattered deep within,
he wants to fix her soul.
She's picking up the pieces,
so he can make her whole.

Disturbance

To end, and to begin
is the process within.
When beginning before the end,
there is turmoil and sin.

Emotions and confusion,
seep out to all parties.
Fear and desperation,
results of being foolhardy.

Swimming in the middle
fighting for the other side.
Spinning in circles,
yet refusing to use the guide.

Does the love in your heart,
outweigh the hollowness?
Will you ever be saved
while on this erring quest?

To end, and to begin
is the process within.
When beginning before the end
there's turmoil and sin.

Crucible

Pain within empty guts
is eating at his soul.
His life is falling apart,
I'm not helping to make it whole.
Choices are out of his hands,
deceiving his love has been.
Afraid of what's to come,
not seeing around the bend.
My heart is rent in two,
watching his world be destroyed.
I want to make it better,
so his life can be enjoyed.
The love that we do share,
is strong, and oh so true.
No matter what's to come,
never forget that I LOVE YOU.

Turmoil

Blinking back the sky
reflecting deep inside.
The twinkle of yesterday
has shriveled up and died.

If tears could create anew,
a life she'd possess with pride.
She'd be a boat upon a river,
savoring the beautiful ride.

Yet daily pains do stab,
creating havoc in her soul.
She wonders at this moment,
will she ever see her goal?

Balm

I wish right from the start
that you were not so far.
You sitting next to me
with eyes that I can see.
Your arms around my waist,
my heart you set in place.
Your scent revives my soul,
from all that's taken a toll.

Vow

The note, the beat,
rising passion,
within us.
The emotions, the want,
the need,
as we throw away all fuss.
The rhythm pulsing
between our souls,
pulling our hearts
together.
The look, the love,
in our eyes,
as we realize,
it's forever.

Him – 10W

My eyes closed
and yet opened
deep within his soul

Lambent

I wish upon a star,
that wishes back to me.
It sees what's in my heart,
and who I'd like to be.
The sparkle touches me,
infused throughout my core.
The energy it brings,
will help my mind to soar.
I wish upon a star,
that wishes back to me.
It sees what's in my heart,
and who I'd like to be.

Hunger – Senryu

Her sweat is his heart
They glisten off each other
Passion, love, sex, forever

Sinking

My insides are mush
My brain cannot compute
The stress of each emotion
Has rendered my soul a mute
Each day that passes by
Each trial stacking higher
Has pulled me down so deep
Into this dark and murky mire

Assassin – Senryu

Breath of my life force
Disintegrating quickly
Stress is a joy killer

Duel

The outward fight of the struggle,
subtle stabs, and pulls.
Desperate fear of impending loss,
as you try to claim the heart
of your dreams.
Head-on collision for one.
Slow methodical hope for the other.
As the heart stands alone,
pulled from opposite ends.
Weighted heavily by suffocated lungs,
the heart is rendered immobile,
useless for either one.
As the morbidity rate increases daily.

Molten Love – Senryu

Lava through my veins
Craving your passionate touch
Seen within your eyes.

Bite – Senryu

The kiss of passion
Licking upon my hot skin
Quaking in shivers.

Gravity – 10W

His love fell
from his eyes
deep into
my soul

Beautiful Confusion

He trusts me with his being,
a heavy responsibility.
The weight and sadness of his heart
is literally killing me.

He's sacrificed it all,
in hopes of a better dream.
He's counting on my love,
throughout all this crazy scheme.

My love is his in full,
with complicated tangles.
So many trials ahead,
I hope that I can wangle.

My heart will always be his,
of this I am most certain.
No matter the distance between,
he will always be "my person".

Time will unveil the answer,
to this interlaced partnership.
Where love and passion lay,
and our bleeding hearts do drip.

Grounded – 10W

He loves her so deeply
she's rooted to the ground

Soul Deep – 10W

He fits in my heart
perfectly safe,
until another time.

Shield – Senryu

The vultures swoop in
At the mere hint of his pain
Stop and heal his heart.

My Protector

He breeds in me a sense
of security I've never known.
A protective shield,
wrapped around me in his presence.
Love vibrates, glistening
off my skin when his eyes
bore into mine.
Volumes are spoken without
one word leaving his lips,
building in me
a love and warmth
to last an eternity.

Focus

The stress and worry
within your heart.
Sets the tone each day
for how it starts.
Lift your head high
and clear your eyes.
I'll be by your side
till the day I die.
Together we'll find
the way it should be.
A time in life, when it's
just you and me.

Ponder

Peer inside, just take a peek.
Of all your deeds, and what you seek.
Are you at peace with what you feel,
or are there moments left to steal?

Heaven

He comes toward her with the
passion, desire,
and the intensity of a Learjet.
Sweeping her up into
his want, his need,
his craving for her body and soul.
Consuming her every breath, as she melts
into one with his strength,
his love, into a place
she can finally call home.

P.S. Rowland

Fractions

The morning after a
realization is the most
sobering of all time.
Was it real? Was it a dream?
Was it a shooting star,
amongst the skies?
Was it the sun that
went down, burning
slowly deep within your soul?
Morning light plays tricks
upon the evening's memories.
Leaving your mind in a whirlwind
of decisions, and doubt.

Yo-Yo – 10W

The shift within his energy
plays games in
my heart

Lukewarm – Senryu

Stone cold against me
I crave fire in my core
miserable love

Osmosis – 10W

The fear and anxiety
in his viscera
shattered my soul.

Soulmuch

He loves me
with the gentleness
of a flower,
and the fierceness of a
warrior

P.S. Rowland

Double Nickels

Double nickels wise and true.
Complications that make me blue.
Integrity tested throughout my soul.
It appears as though I've lost my goal.
Ripples of passion against my heart.
Am I headed for a brand new start?
I gaze around at all I see.
I wonder what is wrong with me.
The toll it takes is wearing me down.
I speak the words, do you hear my sound?
Thunder in his soul as he looks at me,
rattles my cage, and then sets me free.

Reverse Black Widow – Senryu

Tangled in his web
The struggle is not in me
Keep me forever

Grasshopper – 10W

As you pass by
your spirit
jumps into
my heart

Cleansing – Triolet

He kisses places in my soul
And gently peels back each layer
Removing those taking a toll
He kisses places in my soul
The mystical healing he does
Calms and quiets the painful buzz
He kisses places in my soul
And gently peels back each layer

Voltaic – Triolet

His love for her is oh so right
His energy driven into her
The combustion has changed her life
His love for her is oh so right
His touch brings quivers to her soul
Tremors ripple from head to toe
His love for her is oh so right
His energy driven into her

Limitless – Senryu

Come hither, please touch
My heart is yours forever
The future is ours

Tutu – Triolet

Stardust fringes her every step
Her beauty bestowed on many
Her twinkle calms, her heart pulls in
Stardust fringes her every step
Entangled you are in her soul
Enveloped into her being
Stardust fringes her every step
Her beauty bestowed on many

Vision – 10W

Pray for me
that I may
see through
to light

Leather & Lace

Standing on the street
his shoulder brushes mine.
He reaches down to take
my hand, and I am lost in time.
No one exists as we
cherish this touch.
My heart is racing,
I love him so much.
I belong in his arms,
and deep in his heart.
He gave me his soul,
when all this did start.
The deeper we go
into this beautiful mess.
Brings love, joy and passion,
and complete happiness.

Blind Touch – 10W

My desire flares
as he touches me
with his eyes

Serenity – Senryu

Kiss me with your eyes
touch my every desire
calm my restless heart

Rapture – Triolet

He takes her love into his heart.
Where lost she is in ecstasy.
He holds her close so deep inside.
He takes her love into his heart.
The passion within is endless.
As the stars burst between their souls.
He takes her love into his heart.
Where lost she is in ecstasy.

Kinesics – 10W

Heat singed my essence
from his desire
floating towards me.

Complete – Triolet

My love for him deepens each day.
He pieces me back together.
His heart in me is here to stay.
My love for him deepens each day.
He makes me free to be myself.
I feel whole within his embrace.
My love for him deepens each day.
He pieces me back together.

Hearken – Senryu

Ears that listen well
Benefit from words spoken
Deaf ears fare badly

Hopelessly Devoted – Triolet

Take me deep into your heart please.
My soul cannot live without you.
You breath, does cause my existence.
Take me deep into your heart please.
Our love is firm in conviction.
At worse it's the best addiction.
Take me deep into your heart please.
My soul cannot live without you.

Frost Bite – Senryu

The chill around me
Comes long blonde hair, and witchlike.
Ice queen at her best.

Calculating

Her mind keeps working the solution.
Working the problem to her benefit.
The equation is difficult to reach.
To equal the sum she desires.
Never give up on the puzzle.
Persistence will bring in the choice.

Heart Throb – Senryu

The beat inside me
Comes from within his being
Rock me forever

Renewal

The stars fell
to her shoulders,
as worries
melted away,
drizzling slowly
down her body
making her glow.

Comfort – Triolet

I hear his voice, it speaks to me.
It touches deep, and love I see.
His warmth surrounds my every cell.
I hear his voice, it speaks to me.
His touch undoes all my worries.
In his chest my face I bury.
I hear his voice, it speaks to me.
It touches deep, and love I see.

Scorch - Senryu

His lips are steamy
His touch has me on fire
He burns me to ash

Enliven

Kissed by the angel himself.
He blesses my soul with passion.
Awakened only by his
look, word, touch,
as he makes my heart his own.

Rhythmic Love – Triolet

My love of hearts is deep inside.
His beats for me so full of pride.
His touch tells all without a word.
My love of hearts is deep inside.
What hearts do say is more than words.
Emotions flow till lines are blurred.
My love of hearts is deep inside.
His beats for me so full of pride.

Butterfly Kisses – Senryu

Deep blue pools of love
Lapping against my body
Drowning in his eyes

The One

The one who sees inside,
yet doesn't hold it to himself.
The one who feels the words,
although left upon the shelf.
The one who takes the time
to make you feel worthwhile.
The one who misses nothing,
which causes you to smile.
The one who loves your knowing tells,
and makes your life a fairytale.
The one who caught your eye,
although clear across the room,
shooting your heart sky high
until it lands upon the moon.
The one who breathes for you,
causing life itself to be.
Is the one to whom you say
"Yes" when he says
"Please marry me."

Falling Into Place – Triolet

I'm shattered from all that has been.
The changes felt deep in my skin.
You are the glue that makes me whole.
I'm shattered from all that has been.
Your soldering eyes are healing.
You sense my internal feelings.
I'm shattered from all that has been.
The changes felt deep in my skin.

Soothing – 10W

The chaos inside me
Needs consistent calmness
And peaceful love

Fragility

I wish that he can see,
all he does to me.
His moods affect my soul,
and greatly take a toll.
In order to survive,
and keep my soul alive.
Balance is the key
to maintain my fragile chi.
Please keep this thought in mind,
before placing me behind.
Your words, thoughts, and actions,
can cause me dire infractions.
I want this all to last,
not have it be my past.
So consider my welfare first,
before my life is all but dirt.

Sated

It's a mutual
love affair
of the eyes,
mind, heart,
and soul.

Perfect Storm

I hear myself echo within.
Shaking my core down to my skin.
Strength and power are mine today.
How I wish it was here to stay.
Wax and wane my energy moves.
Stability I can then prove.
Endless supplies of you would do.
Without your love I move like glue.
Infused with your intensity.
Unleashes me, and sets me free.

Revive

Tiredness has
seeped into my bones.
Like driftwood, dried out,
left to decay.
Till a day when I am spied
by another.
My beauty, and worth,
are in his eyes.
Gathered into his arms.
I have been repurposed.

"When" – Senryu

The light of his eyes
Speaks trueness of love to her
The answer is, "When"

A New Song – Triolet

Passion, heat, intenseness please give.
Press it to me, so I may live.
Rise above my body, my love.
Passion, heat, intenseness please give.
Your touch I crave forever long.
Next to me as you sing our song.
Passion, heat, intenseness please give.
Press it to me so I may live.

Shilly-Shally

I am floating between,
two worlds.
While not living life
at all.
Afraid to rock the boat,
where others
take the fall.
I fool myself with
delusions,
where happiness does dwell.
While choking on the water,
as I drown
deep in the well.
Time is not my friend,
as I procrastinate
my course.
My heart and mind
do differ,
as I select the
proper source.

In Pieces – Triolet

Matters of the heart stab deeply.
The pain is there for all to see.
She's dying inside so sweetly.
Matters of the heart stab deeply.
Her confusion breeds fear and pain.
There is so much to lose and gain.
Matters of the heart stab deeply.
The pain is there for all to see.

Spirits – Triolet

Bodies brush while souls do ignite.
The pull is strong, so we don't fight.
Your eyes seek mine, and know my plight.
Bodies brush while souls do ignite.
You're in my head and heart as well.
I cannot break your casted spell.
Bodies brush while souls do ignite.
The pull is strong so we don't fight.

P.S. Rowland

Wanderlust

Floating across the trees,
I dream and dance inside.
Of all the little pretty things,
you give me through your eyes.
The feelings oh so deep,
which kiss my wanting heart.
I flutter through the clouds,
and give you my best parts.
The thought of us does come,
flirting with my mind.
I know it's not a dream.
I'm waiting for our time.

Transform – Senryu

Hit with his blue sea
Deeper than the depths of hell
Paradise reborn

Insanity – Triolet

Pressed are my lungs, no breath in sight.
Death is near, I've caused my own plight.
Choices I've made, shatter your sphere.
It breaks my heart, I see your tears.
Selfishness has landed me here.
I hate myself, and these past years.
Pressed are my lungs, no breath in sight.
Death is near, I've caused my own plight.

Exposed – Triolet

Packed and exposed, seen by many.
All she has left, is a few pennies.
She wanders in her mind so lost.
Packed and exposed, seen by many.
She has the dream, or so she thought.
Though loneliness, is all she got.
Packed and exposed, seen by many
All she has left, is a few pennies.

Babydoll – Triolet

I don't know what he wants from me.
He says I'm all he wants to see.
Kept hidden for his eyes only.
I don't know what he wants from me.
I try my best to be his girl.
The only one that he does twirl.
I don't know what he wants from me.
He says I'm all he wants to see.

United – Triolet

Be the light that shines through others.
Love please give to all your brothers.
Positive vibes float all around.
Be the light that shines through others.
Soften your heart and understand.
Expand yourself and take a hand.
Be the light that shines through others.
Love please give to all your brothers.

Theater Of War

The time is drawing near,
That most mankind will fear
Reflecting on their lives,
Were they foolish and/or wise?
Mistakes are often made.
The pain at times will fade.
Reality caves in,
As we ponder all our sins.
We beg on bended knee,
And God we hope will see.
We did the best we could,
Not always what we should.

Divided – Senryu

Festering my heart
Two slivers inside do ache
Rip myself in two

Cutting – Senryu

Caress her insides
Words touch deep into her heart
Remove thy dagger

Exhaustion – Triolet

Once upon a time her heart glowed.
Love and devotion from her flowed.
Stifled now her feelings are stowed.
Once upon a time her heart glowed.
Emptiness has settled inside.
Where once she lived with open pride.
Once upon a time her heart glowed.
Love and devotion from her flowed.

Good Morning My Love

You are the love of my life,
although a little late.
But the love you give me,
makes you my perfect mate.
From our eyes to our souls,
connected we are.
There's no doubt of our love,
it was made in the stars.
So toss away stress,
and anxiety.
My love for you, is for eternity.
As long as there's you,
there will always be me.
Look in my eyes,
and then you will see.

I hope you enjoyed reading **Cut Both Ways**. I would love to hear from you. Please take a moment to write a review on Amazon, I would greatly appreciate it.

You may contact me via my website at www.psrowland.com

Other Books by P.S. Rowland

"Lest We Forget Life's Passion"

A collection of poetry that probes the intuitive language of the heart - the universal human experiences of love, nature, struggle and faith, through a combination of free verse poetry, rhyme and haiku.

Available on Amazon and Barnes and Noble

Acknowledgements

I'd like to thank all of my readers for your continued support of my work, which made this book possible. To all of you who cherish the love of words, the beauty in poetry, and have both embedded in your hearts and minds.

I'd like to express my gratitude to my family and friends for giving me the encouragement to press forward in my career as a writer. I love you all.

A special thanks to Craig P. Weeks, for being my second pair of eyes and titling many of the poems. It's been fun!

www.ingramcontent.com/pod-product-compliance
Lightning Source LLC
LaVergne TN
LVHW041546070426
835507LV00011B/958